A LITTLE BEFORE TWELVE

A LITTLE BEFORE TWELVE
Cynthia Andrews

Poets of Queens Press
New York, 2021

Designed and composed by Oleksandr Fraze-Frazenko.

On the Cover:
Photo by Kei Scampa.
Design by Oleksandr Fraze-Frazenko.

© All rights reserved. Printed in the USA. No part of this work may be reproduced or used in any form by any means — graphic, electronic or mechanical, including photocopying, recording, taping or usage in information storage and retrieval systems — without prior written permission of the authors, except for brief extracts for the purpose of review of this book.

ISBN 978-1-7351478-2-6

*For My Teacher,
Allen Ginsberg*

CONTENTS

BIOGRAPHY	8
STARBUCKS ON SATURDAY AT SIX	11
IN THE TOWERS	12
THE UPPER ROOM	13
MECCA	14
THE IDEAL CITY	15
WAG THE DOG	16
WE MADE YOU	17
INCOGNITO	18
IT'S NICE TO BE NICE	19
NEWT'S NUKES	21
STRING OF PEARLS	22
SYLVIA PLATH'S REVENGE	23
RUDE GIRL	24
FAMOUS PEOPLE	25
WOMEN'S STUDIES	26
MAGDELENE'S FURY	27
COVER ME	28
SHE CAN TURN HEADS	29
MAKING LOVE	35
A LITTLE BEFORE TWELVE	38
A SPACE IN TIME	39
TALK TO ME	40
YOU WILL MEET A HANDSOME STRANGER	41
HARVEY	42
ALAS IS MORE	43
RIBBON IN THE SKY	44
A SOLDIER'S DAUGHTER NEVER CRIES	45
DADDY'S GIRL	46
FIELD OF DREAMS	47
VICTORIA	48
SAVING SUMMER	49
SEEDLINGS	50
JO-JO	51
EASTER SUNDAY	52
A PIECE OF MY HEART	53
FLORENCE THE FLOREST	54
BABY BOOMER	55
THROUGH THE AWFUL GRACE OF GOD	56
RFK	57
POSITIVELY FIRST STREET	58
IN BACK OF THE REALLY REALLY REALLY REAL	59

THE BEST MINDS OF OUR GENERATION	60
JACK KEROUAC'S DREAM	61
BACK IN THE USSR	62
CALIFORNIA DREAMIN'	63
A COLD MAY IN HELL	64
WHAT IS A WEEKEND?	65
AMNESIA	66
CORONAVIRUS	67
HEY JUDE	68
NOTES FROM ARMAGEDDON	69
ET MAINTENANT MON AMOUR	70
GENTLE ON MY MIND	71
CONSOLATION	72
SOLIDARITY	73

BIOGRAPHY

Cynthia Andrews is a veteran of the NYC poetry circuit, and has had readings in such venues as The Knitting Factory, Cornelia Street Café, St. Marks Church, and The Nuyorican Poets Café, where her performance was one of the first to be archived at Poet's House. She is the author of two chapbooks *Saving Summer* and *Homeless* (The New Press.) *A Little Before Twelve* is her first full collection of poetry. She has been widely published in various literary journals and anthologies, including *ALOUD: Voices from the Nuyorican Poets Café*, *The Voice Literary Supplement*, *The 2020 Beat Poets Anthology*, Long *Shot*, *Red Fez* and *Tribes Literary Journal*. She has been a favored guest poet on cable TV and radio, including Teachers and Writers in the Morning and WBAI New York. Nominated for a Pushcart Prize twice and a finalist for the Downtown Year of the Poet award, she holds an MFA in Creative Writing and resides in Queens, New York.

Some of the poems in this book have been published in slightly different form in the following publications:

Notes from Armageddon previously appeared in Red Fez; Starbucks on Saturday at Sir previously appeared in Red Fez and Nomad's Choir Literary Journal; ***Amnesia*** previously appeared in ALOUD: Voices from the Nuyorican Poets Café anthology, Longshot Literary Journal, -The Brooklyn Review, Downtown Magazine and Stained Sheets; ***Women's Studies*** previously appeared in The Voice Literary Supplement and Longshot Literary Journal; ***Jack Kerouac's Dream*** previously appeared in The Brooklyn Review, Medicinal Purposes Literary Journal, Downtown Magazine, Nomad's Choir Literary Journal, Stained Sheets and The Unbearables anthology; ***Magdelene's Fury*** previously appeared in Scholarpoems, Medicinal Purposes Literary Journal and Nomad's Choir Literary Journal; ***She Can Turn Heads*** previously appeared in Downtown Magazine and Stained Sheets; ***Solidarity*** previously appeared in Nomad's Choir Literary Journal and Medicinal Purposes Literary Journal; ***Newt's Nukes*** previously appeared in Will Fight For Peace anthology and Downtown Magazine; ***Making Love*** previously appeared in In Heat anthology and Downtown Magazine; ***The Ideal City*** previously appeared in Out of This World anthology of St. Mark's Poetry Project and Stained Sheets; ***Victoria*** previously appeared in Tribes Literary Journal; ***Daddy's Girl*** previously appeared in The New Press Literary Journal, Tribes Literary Journal, Nomad's Choir Literary Journal and Downtown Magazine; ***Hey Jude*** previously appeared in Silver Birch Press; ***A Little Before Twelve*** previously appeared in The 2020 Beat Poets Anthology and Global Poemic; ***A Soldier's Daughter Never Cries*** previously appeared in Chronogram Literary Magazine; ***Gentle On My Mind*** previously appeared in Drunk Monkeys Literary Magazine; ***Positively First Street*** previously appeared in The Button Eye Review; ***Consolation*** previously appeared in La Piccioletta Barca; ***Seedlings*** previously appeared in The Queens Gazette.

STARBUCKS ON SATURDAY AT SIX

When the days grow long and old too quickly for their own good and I feel summer coming on, I sit in a café just a short mile from the former site. I sit and let the time go by and always see someone who looks like the guy who searched and searched for his son's remains until he found them. He's got a grey beard but doesn't look more than fifty, and brings me back to the memory of that day when I sprinted down Broadway toward Canal Street and ducked into a coffee shop giving away sandwiches and coffee, and then I cried in the bathroom for ten minutes straight with my hands clutching the sink. He was the guy sitting in a corner and alone, just like I am now, and the owner lady told me he's down there day and night, even after having found his son. Two girls on a Saturday shopping spree coming from Soho sit across from me. Michael Kors and Juicy Couture fill their heads. Thank God it stopped raining.

IN THE TOWERS

In the Towers I am thirty-something, designer suits and absolutely perfect. In the Towers I am in demand. In the Towers I am indispensable. I am indescribably ambitious. In the Towers I am climbing up the proverbial ladder of success and waiting for nobody. In the Towers I say what I mean and mean what I say, and change out of grimy sneakers to exquisite black high-heeled pumps! In the Towers I race to my desk every morning with my first cup of coffee and gourmet muffin. In the Towers I dream in vacant office with Money Magazine in one hand and The Complete Poems of Emily Dickinson in the other. In the Towers I am French manicure. (In the Towers I've just got to get my degree!) In the Towers I am "A" student. In the Towers I am legal eagle! In the Towers I am just engaged. Just married. Just divorced. In the Towers I am soft soft spoken and Christmas parties at the Waldorf. In the Towers I am Ralph Lauren model and designer sunglasses. In the Towers I watch the sun go down every night and raise it on high in the morning.

THE UPPER ROOM

I have just gotten this job as a temp and I am sitting at my small desk in front of a huge window staring at the biggest American flag I've ever seen stretched across the New York Stock Exchange which is surrounded by New York Police, Secret Service guys in aviator sunglasses and what look like little green men in military uniforms running around and hopping into their jeeps. It's a small group in this department. They have just come back from the far reaches of upstate New York, and before then some remote town in New Jersey. It is February 2002 a good four months after 9/11 and I can still see the smoke rising out of the ashes of the World Trade Center every morning and every night walking back and forth from the subway. There's a girl with a sweet southern accent and black as night skin who suddenly says that she would not be at all surprised if Osama Bin Laden himself was walking around the block in a Gucci business suit this very minute, and then the man sitting across from me suddenly says that he is absolutely positive that the New York Stock Exchange will be bombed within the week and we're all going to die anyway so what does it matter who's walking around the corner, and then the girl with the sweet southern accent asks me to join a prayer group in the conference room a floor above us on our lunch hour, but as it turns out I just can't make it because I was really hungry that day and ended up buying myself a huge hero sandwich from the corner deli which I ate at my small desk in front of the huge window while staring at the biggest American flag I've ever seen.

MECCA

When all was perfect and completely sublime and
the lives of the masses in perfect rhyme, It
happened so suddenly on this perfect day and
made a gorgeous blue sky turn a deathly grey.

On a Tuesday it was that no one would suspect
that a Tuesday would turn such an ugly mess,
So I turned to the east and I turned to the west
where once God came to increase and bless.

My hands felt numb as I raised them to the sky
lest I cower to the ground like an animal dies,
Where once I bathed in the heat of bright light
now fell a darkness upon all that is right.

My friends jumped fast to hasten their deaths
three thousand and counting went to their rest,
Where stood the Twin Towers proud and high
now an iron cross and their ashes lie.

I bear witness now to my great city's fall when
fell such evil upon us all,
Where once I wore silk and fine tweeds and gold
and walked with pride on the streets of cobblestone.

The murderers died too for their special cause
while killing themselves like some expendable loss,
But no gold, nor oil nor dollar nor gem could equal
the lives of my three thousand friends.

THE IDEAL CITY

It's up on a hill, all shining and majestic like a diamond to be looked at but never worn. To step on its ground will make you wiser than the greatest sage and more loving than even you thought possible. It's a place where dreams are real and life is a manufactured reality of yesterday's thoughts. It's not Paris or New York. It's the ideal city, but don't run. It will always be there.

WAG THE DOG

They definitely breathe a different
kind of air. The liars of the world
construct their words in expert
movements: heresy, gossip,
propaganda, just to name a few. It's all
the same to you and me, but in the end
it's a taboo or politically correct, and
then you end up stuck in a corner and
standing out like a sore thumb reading
a book in a café and "wasting trees,"
while everybody else is downloading!

WE MADE YOU

We made you. We gave you. We took from you. We stole from You. We left you. We lied to you. We got you where we want You. We made you. We love you. We hate you. We are with You. We are without you. We are against you. We are for you.
We starve you. We pay you. We hire you. We feed you.
We deprive you. We kiss you. We hurt you. We venerate you.
We denigrate and demean you. We loathe you. We adore you.
We sing your praises. We list your vices like anxious vultures.
We run for cover. We are out in the open.
                                            (We are out of the closet!) We are right behind you! We have you now. We lost you forever. We bring you up. We bring you down. We find you. We lose you. We keep you as we want you. We made you. We are not God, but who asked you.

INCOGNITO

The books they want to read are easily
and quickly removed from the shelves or
burned, as though they are the brutes of
this world, and not the poets.

Suicide is encouraged.

Cigarettes are stolen, as are money, clothes
and even lipstick as part of a campaign for
healthy eating and a cleaner environment!

All religion is frowned upon, and of course,
poetry is banned.

No one is allowed to dream for longer than
thirty minutes without being chased out of
cafes and labeled a "subversive." It is forbidden
to write about love, eroticism or political
choice without being called "salacious" and
"dangerous."

It would seem someone is deathly afraid
that all their power will suddenly be taken
away with a couple of strong verses in
iambic pentameter.

IT'S NICE TO BE NICE

Nice is nice and ice is ice and nice I say thrice is even nicer than nice and whilst we wait for the nice to be nicer than nice like ice it is for the n ice like ice it is for the nice is not feisty or miserly or likely to heist your heart in icy breaths of terror and whilst we wait for the nice to be nice again and again and again ice is still ice and nice is nice for the sake of it for the sake sake sake sake sake sake of it for the sake of ice is ice and nice is nice and could be anything anything anything at all but whilst we wait and wait and wait and wait for the ice to be nice and nice is nice and ice is ice but whilst we wait and wait and wait and wait still longer and wait even longer for the nice to be nice and the ice to be nice again the nice can be nice to the ice whilst we wait for the ice to be nice in the PC logos and logic of exaggerated truths and lies upon lies whilst we wait and wait and wait and wait whilst we wait and wait and wait and wait and wait for the nice for the nice the nice the nice to be to be to be to be nice nice nice nice NICE again!
WAIT for the nice to be nice again and again and AGAIN and

again and again then ice is still ice and nice is still nice but the nice can be nice to the ice and the nice can be can can can can can (YES IT IS ABLE!) to be NICE NICE NICE
NICE NICE AS NICE AS APPLE
PIE NICE!

can can can can be nice (oh very nice!) nice nice as nice
nice as nice as nice as pie as apple pie just as nice as
nice as nice as nice as pie as apple pie nice to the ice to
nice to the ice nice to the ice nice to the ice nice as apple
pie to the ice the nice can be nice is still ice but the nice
can be can can can can Can CAN
(certainly!) can be nice to the ice.

NEWT'S NUKES

Those people over there are eating yogurt (and a mango!)
                                           for breakfast.
They must be from California.
All waiters in coffee bars are Gay.
Any book by D.H. Lawrence should be burned immediately.
Isadora Duncan was a dirty, vulgar slut.
Anybody who dances without panties is a dirty, vulgar slut.
Anybody who writes "sex" poems is a dirty, vulgar slut.
All sex poems should be burned immediately.
All women who wear makeup and tight jeans are dirty, vulgar sluts.
All women who wear makeup and tight jeans should never
                                           be allowed to
work with the opposite sex. (It's too distracting!)
Walt Whitman was a dirty old man who wrote sex poems.
Leaves of Grass should be burned immediately.
The only good book is the Bible (King James version).

STRING OF PEARLS

A string of pearls is a thing of beauty and always makes a definite statement about the woman who's wearing it. Every time I see wives of presidents and such wearing a long strand of pearls I have to think of how perfect these wives must be too, and how expertly defined their lives must be, just like each pearl she is wearing and how they must glisten each time she opens the box, and any time she needs to feel beautiful they will always be there waiting for her in their perfect little velvet box.

SYLVIA PLATH'S REVENGE

I suppose she thought that she could
get under the skin of every female
poet that came after her, but she
cannot! I ain't no Confessional Poet!

Stanzas of bitter guilt-trip diatribes and
wimpy, sappy "sacred" suicide poems!

I don't break like a cheap piece of wood,
and I don't cry like a baby when it rains!

I ain't no Confessional Poet and
Sylvia Plath ain't got nothing on me,
and besides she was much taller.

RUDE GIRL

She leaves tiny tips or nothing at all. She despises anything that even remotely resembles "PC." She will always walk up the steps that are only meant for the crowd walking down. When she is in a conversation with someone who speaks too slowly she will always interrupt them to ask where the bathroom might be. When she is of the opinion that someone is an intolerable bore she will proceed to imitate them even if they are still in the room. When she is on a date with someone who turns out to be an insufferable dud she will suddenly begin to recite lines from *Gone With the Wind*, such as "Oh Rhett!" and "There's always tomorrow!" Whenever her coffee costs more than one dollar, nine times out of ten she will pay the difference in pennies.

FAMOUS PEOPLE

There's a groovy lady I met at the
corner café who looks exactly like
Joanne Woodward! We ended up
having a lengthy and very
interesting conversation about Paul
Newman for a couple of hours.

The other day I stopped at the neighborhood pizza
place and as soon as the owner turned to face me
and stopped kneading the dough, I knew instantly
that I was facing Barak Obama! He said, "Yes I
can! I can have two slices!"

I just hope that Hillary Clinton will still be at
the supermarket to ring up my groceries!

WOMEN'S STUDIES

She said: I am a rich trust fund baby, so you'd better get out of my way. I am from the
land of white homes and neat fences around each four comer, so if you know what's
good for you, you'll ssssssssssssssssssssssssstay out of my way!
I am the doll, she said, they played with in adolescent leisure and by the time it
all ended, I was the flesh-toned goddess of Vidal

Soon highlights and French couture and the answer to the world's problems of disease, alienation and wars and when I fuck I graciously accept the reward with a smile because I am always in control of my world. I am the finest you can find anywhere.
I am a reproduction of generations you could not fathom in your wildest dreams of gold and god and education from my lawn I can see summer undressing slowly in a morning heat, and I think then, I must be in some kind of a dream moving slowly into night and disappearing over roof tops. I've got time on my hands that you could not fathom.
1 could read *The New York Times* when I was four, and when I am fucking I dream of gold and god and the white summer heat of endless hours that you could not fathom in your wildest dreams so if you know what's good for you you'll

KEEP OUT OF MY WAY!

I said: I am a descendant of generations that you could not fathom in your wildest
dreams, and when I fuck I AM the gold and the goddess of all creation. I am the finest you could find anywhere and

I could read *The New York Times* when I was three!

So you'd better

KEEP OUT OF MY WAY!

MAGDELENE'S FURY

I thought about going down to the Galilee on
a morning when I couldn't be seen, and
washing in the cool drift, cold and clean.

I thought about staying when the sun rises high
and riding the waves that reach up to the sky.

All my nights haunt me before dawn hits the door while
a lamp rocks in shadows and my eyes are too sore, to
close by themselves when the last one leaves and I'm
crawling to bed on my knees.

But the sea of Galilee opens its tide and allows a
child to quietly cry, for the moments of touching
that have gone and left and the miserable joke of
where they slept.

so I ran into the morning just to breathe in a way
and walked with the sun on the shore of the day,
and hid through the night while I slept in the sand
with the Galilee's water touching my hand.

As I watched the sky regain its light and a
child of darkness fade with the night, I
leaned on a rock and rested my head and
listened to the shell of the innocent dead.

And lingered on the ocean of fears and regret
while the Galilee's tide helped me forget.

COVER ME

Let me slide my legs around yours. Let me slip my tongue between your lips. Let me sing a while like Billie Holiday and let me drag it on until at least midnight. Let me rant on for my own good. Let me whisper sweet poems in your ear before you sleep. Let me take all my clothes off and stay with you tonight

SHE CAN TURN HEADS

She can walk into a room and turn heads. She can walk into a room and turn heads. She can turn heads when she walks into a room. She can turn heads. She can turn heads. She can turn heads when she walks into a room. She can turn heads turn heads turn heads turn turn turn turn turn turn turn turn heads heads heads heads(!) when she walks into a room. She can turn heads turn turn turn turn turn turn turn turn turn turn heads with a smile. She can turn heads with a smile. She can turn heads turn heads tum turn turn turn turn heads turn heads turn heads with a smile just a small sweet simple scintillating smile. She can turn turn turn heads turn heads turn heads turn heads with a smile, a small sweet simple scintillating smile, just a small, sweet simple scintillating smile and she can turn heads. She can turn she can turn she can turn turn turn turn turn heads turn heads turn heads turn heads with a smile.

SHE CAN TURN HEADS WITH A SMALL SWEET SIMPLE SCINTILATING SMILE.

> SHE CAN TURN HEADS.
>
> SHE CAN TURN HEADS.
>
> SHE CAN TURN HEADS.

She can turn heads with a small sweet simple scintillating single smile and she can turn heads. She can turn turn turn she can turn turn turn she can turn she can turn she can turn heads with a small sweet simple scintillating single smile and she can turn heads! She can walk into a room and turn heads. She can walk into a room and turn heads. She can walk into a room and turn heads turn turn turn turn turn turn turn turn turn turn TURN HEADS with a smile a smile a smile a smile a

smile just a smile just a smile just a small smile just a small
smile just a smile a smile a smile a smile just a small sweet
smile a small sweet smile a small sweet smile a small sweet
smile just a smile a smile a smile a smile a small sweet
simple simple simple scintillating single smile
and she can turn heads!

SHECANTURN HEADS WITH A SMALL SWEET SIMPLE SS
SSSSSSSSSSSSSSSSSSSSSSSSSSSSSCCINTILLATING SMILE AND

SHE CAN TURN HEADS! SHE CAN TURN HEADS WITH A
SMALL SWEEEEEEEEET SIMPLE
SSSSSSSSSSSSSSSSSSSSSSSSSSSSSSSSSSSSSSSCINTILLATING
SINGLE SMILE AND SHE CAN TURN HEADS!

She can turn heads with a small sweet simple scintillating
single smile and she can turn heads! She can turn heads with a
smile, just a small

    SWEET SINGLE
SSSSSSSSSSSSSSSSSSSSSSSSSCIMILLATING SINGLE SMILE! SHE
CAN TURN HEADS!

SHE CAN TURN HEADS WITH A SMILE JUST A SMALL SWEET
SINGLE
SSSSSSSSSSSSSSSSSSSSSSSSSSSCINTILLATING SINGLE SMILE
AND SHE CAN
TURN HEADS. SHE CAN TURN HEADS. SHE CAN TURN HEADS
SMILE CAN TURN HEADS SHE CAN TURN HEADS SHE CAN
TURN HEADS WITH A SMILE SHE CAN
TURN HEADS WITH A SMALLSWEETSIMPLE
SSSSSSSSSSSSSSSS
SSSSSSSSSSSSSSSSSSSSCINTILLATING SINGLE SMILE AND SHE
CAN TURN
HEADSSHECANTURNHEADSWITHASMILEASMILEASMILEAS
MILEAJUSTA

SMALLSWEETSIMPLESSSSSSSSSSSSSSSSSSSSSSSSSSSSSSSSSS
SSSSSSSSSSSSSSSS
SSSSSSSSSSSSSSSSSSSSSSSSSSSSSSSSSSSSSSSSSSSSSSSSSSSSSSSS
SSSSSSSS

  CINTILLATINGSINGLESMILEANDSHECANTURNHEAD S.
SHE CAN TURN HEADS WITH A SMILE AND A DAB OF DIOR.

SHE CAN TURN HEADS WITH A SMILE AND A DAB OF DIOR!

She can turn heads with a smile and a dab ofDIOR! She can turn heads with a smile just a small sweet simple ssssssssssssssssssssssscintillating single smile and a dab a dab a dab a dab a Dab DAB DAB A

  DABDABDABDABA DAB A DAB A DAB A
DABDABDABDABDABADAB A DAB OF DIOR!

SHE CAN TURN HEADS WITH A DAB OF DIOR!

just a small sweet simple tillating single smile and a dabof dab Ofdab Ofdab Of

A DAB OF DIOR! SHE CAN TURN HEADS WITH A SMALL
SIMPLE SWEET
SINGLE SMILE AND A DAB OF DAB A DAB
DABDABDABDABDABDAB DAB OF
A DAB OF DAB OF DAB OF DAB OF DABDABDAB OF
SHE CAN TURN HEADS WITH A SMILE AND A DAB OF
Just a dabdabdab a dab a dab a dab a dab A DAB JUST A DAB
DAB DAB DAB A DAB OF

SHE CAN TURN HEADS WITH A SMILE AND A DAB OF DIOR
JUST A SMALL
SWEET SIMPLE SINGLE
SSSSSSSSSSSSSSSSSSSSSSSSSSSSSSSSSCINTILL

ATING DAB OF DAB OF DABOF DABDAB DAB A DAB OF

SHE CAN TURN HEADS WITH A SMILE AND A DAB

Just a smile and Dior a smile and Dior and she can turn heads! She can turn heads with a smile and a dab of Dior. She can turn heads with a smile and a dab of Dior. A dab a dab a dab dabdabdab a DAB OF DIOR — just a small sweet simple single smile and a dab of DIOR and she can turn heads —just a smile and a dab a dab and a smile and a dab a smile and a dab a dab a dab and a smile just a smile and a dab a smile a smile a smile a smile just a small sweet simple single smile and a dab a dab a dab adab a dabadabadab ofDIOR! A SMILE AND A DAB. A SMILE AND A DAB A SMILE AND A DAB a smile and a dab a dab a dab a
Smile and adab of

DIOR!

A smile and DIOR a smile and DIORDIOR and a smile DIOR AND A SMILE A SMILE AND DIOR AND SHE CAN TURN HEADS!
 just a small sweet simple
eau Of eau Of
eau du ofeau
ofeau du eau du eaudu eau du eaudududududududu eau du

SHE CAN TURN HEADS WITH A SMILE AND A DAB OF EAU
EAU eau eau eau eau eua dueaudueadu eau du eau du eau eau eau dudududud eau du

OR!
SHE CAN TURN HEADS!
She's got a head on her shoulders but she's a Head Trip! She can turn heads with a small sweet simple single ssssssssssssssssssscintillating single smile and a dab of eau eau eau eau eau du eau du eau

HEAD TRIP!!!!

She's got a head on her shoulders but she's a head trip a head trip a head head head head a
HEAD TRIP!!!! SHE'S GOT A HEAD ON HER SHOULDERS BUT

She can't speak when she's near him. She loves him but she can't speak when she's near him. She can turn heads with a small sweet simple sssssssssssssssssssssssssscintilating single smile and a dab a dab a dab ofeau eau eau eau eau du eau dududududu diiiiiiiiiiiior SHE CAN

near him.

SHE LOVES HIM BECAUSE HE WROTE HER TWO LOVE POEMS AND HE KISSES SO
GOOD. SHE LOVES HIM BUT SHE CAN'T TELL HIM BECAUSE SHE CAN'T SPEAK WHEN SHE'S NEAR HIM. SHE CAN TURN HEADS BUT SHE'S A HEAD TRIP A HEAD AHEAD TRIP

She hates herself when he tells her it's over (while reciting three love poems which he wrote just for her!)

She hates herself when he tells her it's over (while kissing her passionately and reciting Emily Dickinson)

She hates herself when he tells her it's over but
She hates herself when he tells her it's over (while kissing her neck!)

She hates herself when he tells her it's over (while kissing every finger on both hands!)
She hates herself when he tells her it's over but she can turn heads when she walks into a room.
She CAN TURN HEADS WHEN SHE WALKS INTO A ROOM. SHE CAN TURN HEADS WHEN SHE WALKS INTO A ROOM WITH A SMILE JUST

A SMALL SWEET SIMPLE SSSSSSSSSSSSSSSSSSSSSSSSSSSSSSCINTILLATING SINGLE SMILE AND SHE CAN

TURN HEADS WITH A DABABADAB ADAB A DAB OF EAU EAU EAU

OR! SHE CAN TURN HEADS WITH A SMILE AND A

DAB OF EAU OF EAU EAU EAU EAUEAUEAUEAUDUEAUDU
EAU
DU
EAU

MAKING LOVE

Bad sex. Good sex. Meet me around the corner Sex. Quick sex. Long sex and very very very very nice sex. Shy sex- Brazen (I'll take you with the lights On!) sex. Let's do it with the lights OFF! Sex. Hot sex. Steamy sex. I gotta have you before I burst sex! Train sex. Cab sex. Going down and going up elevator Sex. Let's sit down and have some tea sex. Loving sex. Hating sex. (It's all in a day's work!) kind of sex. Easy sex. Crazy sex. Sweaty and grimy and dirty kind of sex. I just want to slide up and down you sex! Take off your bra and I'll take your panties sex! You've got a lot of nerve sex! Neat sex. Messy sex. I am all yours and ONLY YOURS kind of sex. Happy sex. Sad sex. I just can't get it on unless you do THAT sex. Love sex. Loving sex and let's just do it AGAIN sex! Before sex. After sex. I'm always taken for granted sex. I'm always the user sex. I'm a fool for love sex. I'm just the kind of person you'd say that to sex! What do you take me for sex?!? I mean low low low low and lower still kind of sex! I mean really much much much much much lower than even that kind of sex! No I want it like this sex. NO I want it like that sex. No I want it like this like this like this like this sex. I want it fast sex. I want it slow sex. I want it fast sex. I want it slow sex. I want it fast fast fast fast fast fast fast fast sex. I want it slow real real really really slow. Slow slow slow slow slow slow slow slow sex. Slow slow slow fast fast fast slow slow slow fast fast fast fast faster faster. Go FASTER! I love you sex. I hate you sex- I love you sex. I hate you sex. I bet you said that just to get me into bed sex! Poetic sex: "My God, your breasts are like birds in flight!" kind of sex. I love love love you and I hate hate hate hate you but I really love love love love you with all my heart and I really
Love love love love love you especially when you're doing THAT sex! Just let me. Let me let me let me let let let let let me

Do it sex. Just let me do it. Just let me do it. Just let me do it. Just letmedoit just just just just just just just letmedoit, sex and I know just just just how you like it sex! Just let me do it sex. Just let me do it kind of sex. I'll love you forever sex, just please please please put it put put it in NOW!!!!!! Skin on skin spontaneous kind of sex like spontaneous combustion kind of sex! Like I finally I finally finally I finally feel your ... between my legs kind of sex! I just want to rip off all your clothes every time I hear your voice kind of sex! When you speak to me I am mush in your hands kind of sex! (Can we at least find a bed this time, sex?!?) I want you bad sex. I need you in my life sex. I wanna fuck you sex!! Bad sex. Good sex. Messy sex. Grimy sex. Neat sex. Nasty sex. Crazy sex. Poetic sex! I just wanna fuck you sex! Sweaty and dirty and I just wanna slide up and down you sex! I just wanna slide like slide and slide and slide up and up and up upup upupupup and downdown down up and down you sex! You're the Absolute. You're the Truth. You're my only True Love. You're the Only One. Your poems are like epiphanies to my ears! I'll love you FOREVER for saying that! You Temptress! You Angel! You Goddess! Just let me do it sex. Just letmedo it sex. Just let just let me let me let me let let let let let me do it sex. Just let me do it
Just let me do it
Just let me do it
Just justjustjust justst just let Me do it.

JUST LET ME DO IT SEX!

Happy sex. Angry sex. Sad sex. Sappy sex. Long sex. Short Sex. (It's Adequate!) sex. Hot sex. Quick sex. Sweaty sex and very very very very very very very NICE sex. She sex- Brazen sex. Neat sex. Messy sex. Grimy sex. Dirty dirty dirty sex. Clean and proper sex. Hating sex. Loving sex. Cab sex. Train sex. (Let's do it going down now!) sex. I hate you. I love you. I hate you. I love you. I hate you. I love you I hate you I love you love you love you hate hate HATE YOU! I love love LOVE LOVE YOU FOREVER! Love sex. Hate sex. Meet me around the corner sex. Love you. Hate you. Love love you. Love you. Love love love love love you. Meet me round the corner sex. Cab sex. Grimy sex. Hate you. Love you. Neat sex. Love love love love you. Hate you. Love. Hate. Love. Hate. Love love love love love love love you forever kind of sex. Meet me around the corner sex. Love love love love lovelove1ove1ove1oveLOVELOVELOVELOVELOVELOVE LOVE LOVE LOVELOVELOVE- LOVE SEX.

A LITTLE BEFORE TWELVE

I saw you again today in my mind and we made love. You touched my hand and held it for a very long time, just as you have always done. I kissed your neck and the bristle of your cheek and you pulled me toward you. I got out of the subway a little before noon, still thinking of you after the long train ride and surrounded by the smell of roses. I was your muse, conjured up by your own mind as a dream filters through a poem like a goddess of light in a black gauze dress. You stroke my hair slowly and softly and make me giggle and talk poetry long into the morning hours. You touch my hand and hold it for a long time. I kiss your neck and the bristle of your cheek. Your hand suddenly dips into my blouse and I slap it hard, but you make me laugh so much that it really doesn't matter. One of my buttons drops to the floor and I hear it click but I really don't care what's happening around me, except for how good your skin feels on me. I feel your wet lips on mine and can taste the beer you had a moment ago. I saw you again today in my mind and we made love again.

A SPACE IN TIME

No, it is not as bad as when I broke up with him.
 (You know HIM!)
I ended up listening to Carly Simon sing the Spiderweb song
for twenty-eight hours straight (WITHOUT SLEEPING!) until
the downstairs neighbor stuck her head out in the hall and
yelled: PLEASE STOP!!
IN THE NAME OF ALL THAT IS HOLY!
STOP
(Needless to say, of course, this was before headphones!)

So 1 decided instead to play "I'd Like to Change The World" by
Ten Years After ten times in a row, though I was
crying all the time (through my shame and disgust
and anger!) until
I could no longer taste my Hot

Sundae dripping down my chin and then I
thought it would simply be quite unforgivable
not to pay homage to one of the greatest rock
songs ever — so I worked it all off by dancing
around the room (in all my shame and disgust
and anger!) but by the time I pressed re-play I
still couldn't get him out of my mind (you
know — HIM!)
But at least this time I had headphones on!

TALK TO ME

Talk to me. Tell me what a charmer I am. Tell
me what a temptress I'm supposed to be. Talk
to me. Tell me again about the epiphanies of
my poems and whisper to me again of all the
secrets of my soul! Can you please get off that
pose for just a minute and give me a wink and
one of your wise cacks or two? Talk to me.
Let me hear you pushing me to read that poem
you like so much. Take my hand again and
tell me what a charmer I can be and what a
temptress I am and how you dreamed me up
one day in your head, and then there I was,
like magic! Talk to me and come off that pose
once and for all! You know I just keep your
picture there for the fun of it, just a light muse
to glimpse at on my lunch hour and hidden in
the back of my computer — a little cut-out of
a person and not at all real — how could you
be in all this time, so talk to me and give me
one of those sweet kisses on my cheek. I will
not take you out again until twelve noon, and
then you will talk to me again of the
epiphanies of my poems and whisper to me of
all the secrets of my soul, and keep me calm
and true until at least a quarter to five.

YOU WILL MEET A HANDSOME STRANGER

He will lie in great dignity even when he is sleeping. You will kiss him and breathe the delight of Greek gods. He will be neither young nor old and he will have the kind of charisma only great men have, even in their lowest hour. His mind will be free of distraction and always be drawn to something higher. He will be created from a dream you had one night when nothing felt impossible and everything held the truth- You will know it is him by the way he smiles or walks across a room, yet there will always be something strange and lonely about him that you cannot quite name. You take his body to yours and close the harsh light. You kiss his chest and his neck, and softly whisper sweet words to him all night, even after he has won or lost and long after he is sleeping.

HARVEY

The Harvey I knew was not the same imagined rabbit who followed Jimmy Stewart around all day in the movie of the same name. Harvey was a real person who had a bit of a screw loose himself and followed me around all day. I didn't imagine him, but I sometimes thought he was invisible. He bought me dinner and flowers and a new coat, and loved me with all his heart, but I didn't want to believe him. We loved to go shopping on a sale day at the local supermarket, and I liked buying him new shirts. We always watched Doc Martin on TV and I realize now that I can't really live without *him*. To make matters worse, he died on Valentine's Day.

ALAS IS MORE

I always try to write
what truly my heart feels

Like Emily D. I am a poet
with nothing to conceal.

Through our eyes we interpret
what truth there is in rhyme

And make this ugly world
into something sublime.

It seems to me we are so
much alike, I am such a
perfect "square"

Though I am not she, and she
not me. We simply could not
compare!

Alas, our art is much the
same like a game of
truth or dare

When my heart swells
with a passion of the grief
I cannot bear, and

My eyes take in the tragic lives of
human apathy, while standing on
the sidelines like Emily D.

RIBBON IN THE SKY

I have decided not to dance on your grave as I had
told you I would so many years ago, and I won't
waste my time spitting in your eye at your picture either
(though I think sometimes it may be worth the effort, if
only to let off some steam). You've been dead a year and
I only found out last week. How dare you die without
dropping me a line before going into that great unknown!
I guess you still don't miss a beat where I am concerned,
do you? What do you expect me to do cry like a baby
or something? How about a chorus of *Ribbon in the Sky*?
Can you ever forgive me for all those harsh words I had
for you over the phone that day (even if you deserved it!)?
How do you expect me to go on without your telephone
number? Do you really think I'll remember your face or
your touch in another year or two? Do you think I'll recall
your face in the next six months, or the way you touched me in
another year or so?   How do you expect me to go on now?
How can I go on now? How dare you leave me like this!
How can you go and leave me like this? Am I supposed to
go on now? I guess you still don't miss a beat where I'm
concerned do you? I'll forget you in five minutes tops! I'll
throw away anything that could ever remind me of you! I
will not write one poem for you! (this is the last one!) I can
forget you easy in two minutes flat! I won't dance on your
grave as I said I would so many years ago, and that's the best I
can do.

A SOLDIER'S DAUGHTER NEVER CRIES

It feels exactly like the crowded kitchen in
Queens, New York when Queens, New York
was still like country, in the big three family
Victorian when my father's only brother was put
in his grave ten years after my father, and we all
gathered in the big kitchen around the big table
with my father's five sisters surrounding me. It
feels like that now, grieving for you and
yearning for you, a relationship of ten years, and
my oldest cousin asked if I was okay standing at
the grave because I looked so pale. I really
should have married you, how stupid was I? I
sat at the table waiting for all of them: one dark,
one fair, another older than the rest until all five
were there around me. I waited until the coffee
was served to say how much I missed him and
how I wished I could die at seventeen and the
oldest looked at the ceiling and the darkest
looked away and the fairest got up to get more
coffee. I thought at least one of them would lend
me a tear, but they are all children of a war hero
as my father had been, and so I felt the fool with
my face wet, sitting at that table until one of
their husbands began imitating an altar boy in
church earlier who was conspicuously picking
his nose during the service, which of course
made everyone laugh and forget that the worst
had just happened. and then the oldest finally
stopped looking at the ceiling, and I got up to
get myself another cup of coffee.

DADDY'S GIRL

He sold war bonds with movie stars and kept my mother waiting for the big church wedding. He was Third Army all the way, armored division. He ran into a burning tank to save the men in his platoon and was awarded the Silver Star for valor in action. By the time the war was ended he was awarded two Oak Leaf Clusters, three Purple Hearts, the Bronze Star for bravery and a personal letter and citation from General Patton himself. He taught me how to swim by throwing me into the Atlantic Ocean. Every Saturday night when we played Monopoly or Parchese, he made me stay up late for just one more rematch before morning! He brought home crystal ash trays and hand-made clocks from Germany which sat on our mantel for many years. He had a bad knee, a glass eye and shrapnel in every part of his body. He sold so many war bonds he was asked to stay on with the movie stars, which he didn't mind at all. He bought me a Victrola and Elvis Presley records, and taught me how to jitter bug, and every Sunday he would speed down a back road when nobody was around with the radio blaring to the rock and roll station of my choice. He caught malaria in North Africa, which suddenly made a surprise appearance on their honeymoon. He stayed up all night by my crib when one day I had a coughing fit and turned blue. He died of Lou Gehrig's disease when I was seven and never even knew I made the Deans List for three semesters straight.

FIELD OF DREAMS

The minute he looked at me I knew who he was. He looked exactly as I thought he would, only much thinner, and smiled at me when I asked him where he had come from, some army base? He wore a World War II uniform with all his medals pinned to his chest. He said that he had his fill of North Africa and couldn't wait to get a foot into Europe and right through the middle of Germany! He said, "Would you believe it — General Patton just gave me the Silver Star for saving a few of my buddies from a burning tank, but there was nobody else there." I said, "Who died and made you Grouch Marx?" We both sat on a bench in silence looking out on the grey water of the East River, the same river he had swam in as a child before the pollution and the tall condo buildings of the present. He suddenly looked at me and said how proud he was that I had read Chaucer at such an early age, and I said, "Yes, but I'm poor and stupid now." And he said, '"Who died and made you Groucho Marx?" Then his eyes turned grey and cloudy like the water and he suddenly asked me if this was heaven, and I said "No, it's just Brooklyn."

VICTORIA

He is leaning on his mother's knee in this picture; a tiny
god and future war hero. Does she know even then?
Like a princess or French model dressed in silk and
lace, and pregnant with my Aunt Sophie, does she
know he's a hero? In another thirty years or so he will
still be leaning on her knee at her death, sobbing like
the child he once was in this picture, for Victoria.

SAVING SUMMER

I'm watching you sleep now while you lie in that hospital bed slowly dying. You look like a baby with your mouth slightly open. Do you remember how you'd assault me with sunlight to wake me up by raising all the shades? Do you remember how you'd drag me to Coney Island when you couldn't afford to take me to the mountains those summers after Daddy died, praying it wouldn't rain! How you cried every night, so afraid we wouldn't make it without him. There's a window to the left of your bed but you always ask me what the weather is like outside. Let's hope it won't rain.

SEEDLINGS

On those hot summer nights of my childhood when my father had just gone to be with God, we would all be under one roof of a huge Victorian house with a wrap-around porch and oak floors, which my aunt would polish and my cousin Joseph and I would slip on every night just for fun. He would collect ants in a big glass jar and scare me with them every chance he'd get. Then it would be the same cry from my uncle: "It's Westpoint for you in the morning!" My uncle owned a landscaping business, but when I knew him he worked for the airlines and this was long after he was hunted by the Mob for owing some gambling debt, which nobody knew about until long after he passed away. I still can't garden even though I've read every book on gardening he had. I was the only cousin allowed to read his books because he knew I liked to read. One day I asked him if he liked the Beatles. He said he didn't care about their long hair and liked their music, and from that moment on I knew I'd love him forever. We ended up staying for a long time because my mother did not want to go back home after the funeral. At bedtime my cousin and uncle would sleep out on the porch, and my sister and I would be tucked away in the living room. Every night we'd hear the same thing: "Nobody is allowed to sleep out here but me and my Dad!" And then: "It's Westpoint in the morning!" By the time New Years came and went, we had gone back home to school and the old neighborhood, but there was always a party to go to, and we would always visit anyway at least once a week.

JO-JO

She looks like a rubber doll lying there in that hospital bed, the kind I used to pull and squeeze and manipulate in every way to get what I wanted. She is so still now and hardly moves, and the nurses call her "Jo-Jo" as though she were still twelve years old. She has lost so much weight her wedding ring keeps falling off her finger, but she always did have bigger knuckles than me. My mother looks just like a rubber doll, lying there in that hospital bed, the kind I could always manipulate to get what I wanted.

EASTER SUNDAY

My mother had everything prepared for me – new white gloves, a black patent leather bag and shoes and a little straw hat with flowers in the rim. She even bought me my own blue crystal rosary beads in a velvet case all its own, and there's a clean white handkerchief in my new bag with a "C" embroidered in blue. It was so much warmer in the house since Spring finally came. It's 1962 and six months after my father died, and my mother had finally stopped crying so much at night when she thought nobody could see.

A PIECE OF MY HEART

   Have I lost my mind making homemade chicken soup in eighty degree weather? How can I even think, much less be profound in a hot and humid sweat? Shall I die with a smile on my face listening to Dylan in nothing but a sheer nightgown with earphones on? I lived through Vietnam, but who's counting? Why am I contemplating my own death while singing with Judy Collins and Emmylou Harris? I lost my train of thought when the noise around me suddenly drowned out Janis Joplin, and then decided to switch to Janis Ian. I learned the truth at seventeen — make love not war! I was alive when they shot JFK, RFK and MLK. I always voted for the right man, didn't I? In the rubble of their revolution will they forget that the main idea is to change the world for the better? I shut the music and watch the latest news of the riots against racism and injustice, and I think I will have some of that homemade chicken soup after all.

FLORENCE THE FLOREST

She was known in the neighborhood as "Florence the Florest" and her family had been there for three generations. Everyone knew her because everyone had at least one funeral and wedding in their lives. She had perfect roses. Perfect carnations. The perfect corsage for your prom or birthday. The perfect bouquet for the bride, and even the perfect wild flowers and pink satin ribbons tied around crystal vases. She had unruly thick white hair and wore loose cotton dresses in every season, and was often spotted sipping tea near the window of her store watching the crowd from the subway walk home after a long day. Then one day Florence suddenly announced that she was selling her store and moving to the country! We were all saddened and even slightly disgusted to see her go because soon afterward a café moved in, renovated only slightly to retain that "grunge" look, and attracted the kind of people who ate breakfast at one thirty in the afternoon with waitresses who drank more coffee than their customers. Then came a yogurt shop. Then a Pilates studio. Then a gourmet bagel shop. Then, finally, a bank. I don't think that Florence would have lasted much longer anyway. Too much competition.

BABY BOOMER

Everything I am today is because of Creedence Clearwater Revival. The Beatles. The Vietnam war. Anti-War rallies with Jane Fonda and Tom Hayden. RFK, JFK, MLK and Allen Ginsberg. Twelve years of Catholic school. Twenty-five first cousins and ten aunts and uncles, and huge First Communion, Confirmation and Sweet Sixteen parties! Battle of the Bands dances. Expensive peasant blouses. Greenpoint Brooklyn in the 1960's with no air conditioning! Sitting on my stoop reading Kahlil Gibran, Norman Mailer and Bernadette Devlin by the light of a street lamp on hot summer nights when I was fourteen. Singing Amazing Grace out of my kitchen window while the neighbor across our back garden surprises me by playing his bagpipes! Watching our clothes dry in the wind on the line. Dreaming of Europe and true love. Doing nothing on Sunday afternoons after church but watching old movies with my mother while she knits me a scarf. Pajama parties with my girlfriends and listening to Elton John's "My Song" without stopping for the entire night. Dancing to Cosmo's Factory over and over again with my friends every single day after school.

THROUGH THE AWFUL GRACE OF GOD

At three in the afternoon I wrote a poem about Martin Luther King Jr. who was shot a few months ago. At four Sister took us all to Mass for some ridiculous holy day of obligation. At five I rolled up my pleated skirt like every good Catholic school girl, and talked about the newest Beatles album with my friends. At six I saw Bobby Kennedy on the Evening News with blood oozing out of his brains on a hotel floor in California, and then the usual weather report came on and stories about the cleaner subways to come, and pictures of all the boys on stretchers with blood oozing out of their brains. At seven I was spared doing the dishes and escaped to the living room where I put on the latest Rolling Stones album and danced and sang as loud as I could and played it over and over again until my mother finally said, "I can't stand it anymore!"

RFK

I was a tiny little girl at fourteen, a year before Woodstock. It was a cool autumn day I would never forget because it's my favorite time of year. I had just come from the park reading my revolutionary books: Soul On Ice, The Price of My Soul and Armies of the Night. I was determined to change the world. This was the "Garden Spot" of New York but I still couldn't believe anyone would ever come here, especially not him! (Nobody comes here!) I could hear his voice well enough, but a big goofball kept getting in my way. He had just returned from Mississippi trying to help the poor people there, and California also, fighting for a union. I finally caught a glimpse of his long wavy hair and his right hand constantly pushing it back from his face. He said he was running for the Senate or something and then I really couldn't see or even hear anything more because the big goofball completely blocked my way and all of a sudden, like in a fraction of a second, just like his brother, he was gone.

POSITIVELY FIRST STREET

They say that it is as easy as the moon's reflection in a drop of water to meet the great Buddha himself. I met him once, for a moment or two walking with two big shopping bags down Fourteenth Street and First Avenue in New York. I remember it was the end of August and it suddenly began to rain, and I didn't have an umbrella. I was wearing a short little pink thing, which I bought at the GAP and couldn't afford, but splurged for it anyway. I was thirty-something and crying like I was three, but it was okay because the rain hid most of it. I was walking so fast it was almost a run and when I stopped short our eyes met, and then I recognized him immediately. I was shaking and could hardly speak, and it wasn't really because of the short pink thing or the rain. I just left it all behind me, all the screams and illogical words that people say to each other when it's all over, or they think it's over. The Buddha took my hand now and seemed to know where I'd been, and then he put his other hand over mine and asked me to calm down. He said how much he looked forward to seeing me at school in two weeks. I just stood there in the rain and watched him walk passed me to the corner, going home with those two big shopping bags while I walked so slowly and carefully now in the pouring rain to the subway.

IN BACK OF THE REALLY REALLY REALLY REAL

I remember staring at your naked picture for at least
fifteen minutes at the end of semester party you
always had in that old apartment of yours with the
"new" nineteen-thirty refrigerator you bought from
that little shop on the next block to replace the
nineteen-twenty refrigerator! And now I stare at your
picture on some website for Beat poets. I still haven't
taken your advice to become a Buddhist, but your
voice is always in the back of my mind — "Get
real!" "Get grounded!"
"Janis Joplin is dead!" I'm still not writing
the daily Hai-Ku. The torture remains, and I
think that was your plan! It's been ten years
since you've died and I could finally look at
your picture again, still missing you like
crazy without any idea that could possibly
explain why.

THE BEST MINDS OF OUR GENERATION

Every time I light a candle I think of you
in that dark, cold basement reading Blake
by candlelight and writing your intense
poems while contemplating climbing the
Himalayas, hiking through Europe and
walking on water, of course! And then the
trip across the country with the best minds
of our generation. Every time I light a
candle I think of that day you read me two
poems by Yeats — one when he was
twenty and the other when he was sixty,
and then you suddenly asked me how to
properly pronounce Akhmatova.

JACK KEROUAC'S DREAM

It must be Mexico City,
the hallowed ground
where I can finally rest.
It has to be Mexico City,
the crowning glory, the
end of the rainbow, the
last word, the place
where time stops and the
gods converge. It has to
be Mexico City where
all the secrets are finally
told and nothing is a
whisper anymore. It
must be Mexico City
where all my dreams
become a reality, and as
soon as I'm over the
border, everything else
is history.

BACK IN THE USSR

We would have danced
to the Beatles, you and
I, with a vodka in one
hand and our poetry
in the other. I would
have taught you some

New steps you undoubtedly
never heard of before: go
softly, don't shout and sing
when you can't find the words
to speak your sadness.

How I would have paid any-
thing to have seen you grow
old, the blonde thinning, the
gorgeous smile smothered in
my kisses and your wrinkles

From too much thinking,
and what kind of poem would
you have written for me, for
instance, my dear lonely boy?

Or am I just another poet in
your young life, where
love is the same as a terrible
noose around your neck and

Too much vodka – Oh Sergei
Yesenin, what a contrary little
boy you certainly are, but I will
wait for you anyway in the next life.

CALIFORNIA DREAMIN'

I'm not sure why I'm here or where I came from. It's like I'm in some kind of a dream. There was a door open and I just walked in. The curtains are drawn and there's a fire burning. I am somewhere in California in a place called Pacific Grove and he has just finished writing. It was a long day, he tells me, and his nervous stomach is bothering him and he's got a pain in the back. We speak as though we have known each other all of our lives and not a minute or a mere fraction of a second. Of course, I know who he is and I must tell him how much he looks like the absolute embodiment of everything that is California, or once was. He tells me how people would like to kill him for writing his book. He tells me that he is the only one who could write this book, and that it had to be written no matter what. We listen to the thunderous rain coming down in torrents and for some reason I know that I must go now. I kiss him softly and tell him that the world will look better to him soon. As I head for the door he suddenly says that he cannot wait for the days when he is older and wiser, when he might be able to travel around this great country and write a book about it all, and he may even take his dog Charlie.

A COLD MAY IN HELL

I walk from one end of the street to the next just to get some air, but this thing around my face, this mask is keeping springtime at a distance for a while. They say it will be a year or so before this virus is completely gone, but New York never looked prettier though even that is deceptive. There is a cold chill around every corner, threatening rain. They are not sure where it came from — Europe, Asia or Texas? It makes me feel like I am being followed — a brisk wind whistling and whispering in my ear. I walk faster up the street and a frigid chill runs up through my blouse. I think I will clean out my closet again for the fifth time this month. After all, you're dead now and I am alone. Tomorrow I will not make my bed or wash the dishes. I will read poetry all day and write a poem or two. Maybe it will catch up to me before I reach the door. How fast do you think I can walk down this sidewalk? How many times do you think we've walked up and down this street? We have both memorized every crack in this sidewalk, but will I feel different in an hour or so? Maybe in another life.

WHAT IS A WEEKEND?

I'm stuck inside the four walls of my studio apartment because of the covid-19 virus. I'm in New York City and the disease is everywhere, but it has somehow made me realize what is truly important to me and what I really care about, what is closest to my heart beyond everything else — of course I mean "Downton Abbey!" I make myself a hearty breakfast and then an early dinner, and I look forward to five in the evening when there is yet another blessed episode of "Downton Abbey (Every single day!) Anyway, what day is it? I don't know who I like more — the guy who almost dies at the end of season three, or the cute Irish chauffer revolutionary who marries the youngest daughter who dies at the end of season two. Then there's that tough valet, Bates; who got arrested for killing his wife and then married Anna the maid who was viciously attacked by another (creepy!) valet, who Bates probably did kill but was once again miraculously released from prison and proven innocent, and they all lived happily ever after! I'm so glad there's something in my life that keeps my mind off death.

AMNESIA

Springsteen screams out of the
radio like a cat on fire for a little
of that human touch beyond that
of his steel guitar cutting beneath
the fingers.

It's Saturday, a motionless
afternoon in the heat of late June
blurring my vision to the
immediate only — Springsteen
screaming through the fans.

I am too old now to remember
even last year, a month is a
decade and days play their
games with my brain like short
sarcasms or those brief, cold
sweats after a bad

Like amnesia in a heat spell, I
am lucid only when a certain
word is called like a catch
phrase or someone suddenly
clasping my wrist, and then I
recall a name or a book, a few
words may be tied in string
around my mind, but loosely,
until

I'm back in the dog-day sleep
of mid-afternoon with the
immediate around me like
shrubbery, hard and sharp
and biting at my skin while I
sleep.

CORONAVIRUS

Why have they named the virus Covid-19, as though it were some kind of over-the-counter cough syrup? Why is it also called Coronavirus like the name of that beer? Do early symptoms include blowing up and smelling bad? I don't want to die young! What if I'm the only person left in New York City, or even on the face of the earth? What if everybody dies and leaves me here alone? What if there's another hurricane like Sandy and I'm lying here dying of the Coronavirus? What if I can't move and I have to move to Montana? What if it's too late? Maybe Wyoming's closer! What if I have a fever of one hundred and three and I can't speak to save my life? What if God leaves me here to die?

HEY JUDE

Is it because I've gotten older
that I see everyone playing a
part or speaking their lines as
though we're all on Broadway
and we take a great big bow at
the end of our lives, and
everyone stands and applauds
and bravos and roses in my
arms, or will we all be dead
tomorrow? The rich have all
moved to the Hamptons and
have bought all the remaining
groceries from Brooklyn to
Montauk. Shouldn't I at least
pretend I can see a light at the
end of the tunnel for coronavirus
New York City? When I step
into the morning will they love
me or hate me, and will I be
greeted by wild applause and
roses at my feet? I guess I'll read
myself to sleep with an excellent
book, and maybe if I'm lucky
the last of my leftover chicken
will taste a little better than the
night before.

NOTES FROM ARMAGEDDON

They say Florida will be washed up in just a few years and the entire southeast coastline will disappear. It's April 2020 and I am sitting in the middle of the epicenter of the coronavirus in New York City, and my boyfriend just passed away on Valentine's Day and I know I should have married him. I am in my studio apartment day after day cleaning the floors, washing the dishes and reading my mysteries. I hear my mother, my father and my teacher, Allen Ginsberg talking to me between disinfecting kitchen counters and Roseanne repeats: Don't eat too many sweets! Do some exercise! Write me a Hai-Ku every single day for the next three weeks! Yes, I should have married him. I've got enough food for a month, but what happens in May? Maybe I'll have a chocolate donut now that the floors are dry. Thank God I can say how much I still hate the smell of bleach! It's springtime in New York City, but I still wish I could leave these four letter walls for Disneyland.

ET MAINTENANT MON AMOUR

It is not New York City or Paris in the moonlight and you are not dead. Perhaps it is another war, and even in the aftermath of gunfire we can still smell the enchanting scent of Spring wafting in through the bedroom window. Which lover do I call upon to help me to forget the depravity all around me? What heavenly things shall we do to each other to forget? And what is your name today? (Aren't we getting too old for this nonsense?) Let's just see how it all ends. We already know you are dead. Don't be so shocked at all my brazen honesty! It's only me dreaming of you.

GENTLE ON MY MIND

Sometimes there is nothing more to say. Sometimes I am the only one left in the middle of the world of billions of people. Sometimes I'm Big. Sometimes I'm really really small, smaller than the tiniest bug below God's good earth. Sometimes there is me and only me and nobody else, and sometimes it's where do I go from here? Sometimes it's the same and sometimes it's so different I don't recognize my own face. Sometimes the world is just not here anymore and sometimes you come strutting back into my mind like you never left.

CONSOLATION

The church is dark and quiet
except for a woman who looks to
be about ninety years old,
kneeling and sobbing and
whispering prayers to the icon of
the Madonna, though it's only a
copy of the original back in
Poland. What does it matter
anyway? It's only a month after
the attack and all I can remember
is what a damnable long way it
was to walk from the subway to
the Towers and I was always
late! It is the church where my
Mother first taught me to pray. It is
where I received First Communion, got
married in a solemn ceremony, and
cried with all of my classmates after we
had long graduated from the school,
when our Monsignor suddenly died at
eighty-three. I am back today for just a
minute or two. I bury my face in my
hands and join in the cries and sobs to
the Madonna. When I decide to leave
the sudden harsh light of the outside
 world attacks my eyes as I open the
door, so I stay a little longer in the front
chapel where the angel statues offer
solace for tired travelers.

SOLIDARITY

        I am the only New Yorker in the group with my Annie Hall sunglasses and Cabaret haircut. We are all Americans here, studying at the university in Krakow Poland where Copernicus changed the world and where there's a statue of a poet on every corner. I am the only one who knows the Macy's "after Christmas sale," too many boyfriends and jobs going nowhere. In between classes I am always in the Old Town or "Stary Miast," sitting beside the statues and writing poetry! It is 1978 in the middle of the Cold War, and if you can't afford Venice, this is the place to be: Eurotrash and me, sipping strong coffee and listening to the whispers circling around corners of the winding cobblestoned streets where my grandfather probably walked as an officer in the Polish Cavalry and where my grandmother glanced at him and instantly fell in love. Every morning a woman and her baby

        break into our dining room through the back garden when nobody is watching to steal some milk and bread. Some of the waitresses take notice but nobody says anything. Up the narrow alleys and on every church door there is a sign with the words: "UWAGA!" "UWAGA!" Attention! Attention! The meetings take place in the basement and everyone should attend, with the strange word "Solidarnosc" or Solidarity on every other line. The shoemaker I pass every day has vodka for lunch and swears at the top of his lungs that "Poland will be free again!" A few miles down the road from our dorm is a place called Nowa Juta or "New Town, " created by the Soviet government to be a model of their ideals. There is a huge statue of Lenin in the center of the town covered in obscene graffiti by the locals. The year before, Cardinal Wojtila consecrated the first church to ever be erected there after twenty years of pleading with the Soviets. Last week our class was taken to see a film called "Man of Marble," which was banned in the entire country, with the director of the film interrogated and arrested. We sat closely together and were the only ones in the theater. One of my professors of about eighty years old tells us about the day when he was beginning his career at the university and the Nazis killed his father-in-law in cold blood, along with every other tenured professor for their "subversive" ideas and writing. He asks us to remember everything we've seen and heard, and when we get back home to tell everyone we know in our own words, and in our art and poetry. During the last weekend of the session

                we are taken on a field trip to the mountain town of Czestochowa to see the shrine that everyone is always talking about, the one that grants miracles and the one I've heard stories about since I was a child. It is a painting of the Blessed Mother with her face slashed twice during a war with the Turks. It is mounted on the wood from St. Luke's table. We all take a lot of pictures and I kneel with everyone else. When the painting is finally exposed she makes me cry like a damned baby. She makes everyone lose control. We all weep like children kneeling on a cold marble floor in our designer jeans. I run away from the crowd. I need to be alone. I end up on some balcony outside and the stone feels like a thousand years old. My face is wet and I am holding on to the ancient medieval stone with all my might. She grants miracles if you pray hard enough, so I pray like crazy. I look out passed the summer and try to see more before going back inside but I can't, and yet somehow I know this world will never be the same again and neither will I.

www.ingramcontent.com/pod-product-compliance
Lightning Source LLC
Chambersburg PA
CBHW071319080526
44587CB00018B/3282